A Dorling Kindersley Book

Text Christopher Maynard
Project Editor Jane Donnelly
Designer Karen Lieberman
Deputy Managing Art Editor Jane Horne
Deputy Managing Editor Mary Ling
Production Ruth Cobb
Consultant Theresa Greenaway
Picture Researcher Tom Worsley

Additional photography by Dave King, Cyril Laubscher, Tim Ridley, Paul Bricknell, Susannah Price, Steve Gorton, Philip Dowell

First published in Great Britain in 1997
by Dorling Kindersley Limited,
9 Henrietta Street, London WC2E 8PS

Visit us on the World Wide Web at http://www.dk.com

Reprinted 1997

A CIP catalogue record for this book
is available from the British Library.

ISBN: 0-7513-5513-5

Colour reproduction by Chromagraphics, Singapore
Printed and bound in Italy by L.E.G.O.

The publisher would like to thank the following for their kind permission to reproduce their photographs:

t top, b bottom, l left, r right, c centre, BC back cover, FC front cover

Bruce Coleman Collection: 10-11c; **Robert Harding Picture Library**: 6cr, 6br, 7cl, 7bl, 20-21c; **Image Bank**: Frank Whitney 13br; **Tony Stone Images**: Geoff Dore 12-13c, Mark Lewis 7br, JF Preedy 9br, James Randklev 17br, Paul Rees 8bl, Jerome Tisne 14-15c, Mark Wagner 18-19c, John Warden 8-9c; **Telegraph Colour Library**: FC cb, 14bl, 16-17c, endpapers

Contents

WHY

do seasons change?

Questions children ask
about time and seasons

DK

DORLING KINDERSLEY
London • New York • Stuttgart • Moscow

Seasons change because the Earth tilts. The north leans towards the Sun and has summer, while the south leans away and has winter.

Why is it cold in winter?
The weather turns cold in winter because that part of the Earth leans away from the warmth of the Sun.

change?

**Why are days
longer in summer?**
In summer, the Sun climbs
very high in the sky so, on
summer evenings, it takes
longer for the Sun to dip
down below the horizon.
In winter, the Sun stays
lower in the sky and this
makes the days much shorter.

Why do birds

As the days get shorter and colder in winter, many birds fly away or migrate. They go to places where the weather is warmer and where there is plenty of food to be found.

Why are trees bare in winter?
Snow and strong winds would damage a tree's leaves. So trees

migrate?

Why do some animals sleep in winter?
Sleeping deeply all winter is called hibernation. Animals store fat in their bodies before they hibernate. In this way they survive the cold months when there is little food.

stop sending water to their leaves and withdraw useful chemicals from them. The leaves then fall off.

Why is it dark

The Earth spins like a giant top. When one side faces the Sun it has daytime. The side facing away from the Sun is dark and has night-time.

Why is it hottest at midday?
By midday, the Sun has been warming the Earth for hours, and it is still high in the sky, giving its

at night?

Why do we have shadows?
Sunlight travels in
straight lines. When
it shines on one
side of you,
your body blocks
the light, casting
a pool of shade that
shows your outline.

full heat to the Earth. Once the
Sun begins to sink, the effect of its
rays diminishes, and the air cools.

Why does the Moon change

The Moon shines because it reflects sunlight. As the Moon travels around the Earth, we see different amounts of its sunlit face because the Earth casts a shadow on it. In a full Moon, light is reflected off the whole, round face of the Moon.

Why is the Moon so bright?
The Moon has no light of its own. However, sometimes it reflects the

shape?

Why is the Moon sometimes out in the day?
The Moon may be out anytime, day or night. But in broad daylight, the sky is far too bright to see it. Later in the day, as sunshine fades, the Moon comes into view again.

Sun's light so brightly that you can see well enough to read a book outdoors at midnight.

Why do I only have

Birthdays celebrate the day you were born. This date only comes around once a year. If you've just had a birthday, you'll have to wait a year for the next!

Why is a year so long?
A year measures the time it takes the Earth to go once around the Sun,

one birthday a year?

Why do people get older?
Time can only go forwards. Every minute that passes, we all get a little bit older. The more time that goes by, the older we get. You can see how people change if you look at photographs taken years apart.

which is just over 365 days. A year is always the same because the Earth moves at the same speed.

Why are baby

Spring is when the weather warms up and new plants and grass start to grow. Baby animals have a much better chance of surviving then than if they are born in the winter.

Why does some fruit ripen in autumn?
It takes a whole summer of sunshine for some plants to produce fruit. It is not until autumn

birds born in spring?

Why do some flowers close their petals at night?
Some flowers shut their petals as the Sun sets to protect themselves from the cool night air and from being attacked by night-time creatures. These flowers wait for the sunshine before they open up again.

hat the fruit is fully grown. Tropical fruits ripen all year round – here is no autumn in the tropics.

Why does the time

Earth is always turning, so the Sun begins to light up each part of it at a different time. People set their clocks according to this time. If we travel by jet, we may land in places with different local times.

Why does a plane move so slowly across the sky?
When it flies low over your house, a jet comes and goes in a flash. But high in the sky, it takes

change when we travel?

Why does jet lag make you sleepy?
The world is divided into regions called time zones. Jet lag happens when you arrive in a time zone several hours ahead or behind your own. It can be morning, when your body thinks it's time for bed.

several minutes to pass by. This is because it is far enough away for you to see it fly 20 or 30 km before it is out of your sight.

Long ago, sundials were used to tell the time. Sundials measure the shadow cast by the Sun as it travels across the sky.

Why do clocks have twelve numbers?

There are 24 hours in every day. We count the first half of the day up to 12 noon, and then start again and count to 12 midnight.

sundials?

Why do clocks have two hands?

The long hand moves steadily to mark all the minutes in an hour. The short hand moves more slowly to mark each hour. Some clocks have a third hand for seconds.